INSERT IMAGE OF SELF HERE

this journal belongs to

Write down your intentions for yourself whilst using this journal below.

_____
_____
_____
_____
_____
_____
_____
_____

Message from the Author

Dear Sis,

I am elated that you have decided to invest some quality time with yourself by purchasing this journal.

The aim of this book is to help you explore the woman that you were, are and will be in the future. These wellbeing exercises, poems, meditations, gentle reminders and prints have been designed with thought, love and the desire to help you feel empowered.

Each journal prompt will help you to peel back the layers of your womanhood and identity. Each poem will leave you feeling nourished and visible. Each quote will inspire and awaken you. Each meditation will restore and realign you.

So take your time.
There is no reason to rush through this.

This is your opportunity to pour back into Self, without fear of being judged, belittled and/or fearful. Here is your chance to be exactly *who you are*.

Nadine Plummer

navigate

/nav-i-geyt/ verb

1. To move on, to move over or through
2. To direct and/or manage; taking control of the course/direction
3. To pass over

Standing in your truth is like standing in quicksand, even when others tell you to grab for something to save yourself. Continue to breathe life into the sands of Self. Let it travel along the lineages that you are yet to discover. The small golden crystals may pinch into the soles of your feet but allow those small successions of heat to ignite your drive to stand taller. Expand your chest. Hold yourself. Sink your feet in a little deeper until your knees offer a humbling bow. Do not let the sand swallow you up whole. Surrender yourself into it. Swan dive and forward fold into the layers of your identity.

Don't panic. Just feel. You'll be fine.

LIST 50 THINGS ABOUT YOURSELF THAT YOU LOVE

Gratitude is the Attitude

Use this template to help you keep track of all the wonderful things/people you are grateful for in life.

This could be about all of those big milestones or small stepping stones in the right direction you have made; remember there is no right or wrong sis.

TODAY I FEEL

1

2

3

4

5

6

7

8

9

10

TOMORROW I WILL   I WANT MORE...   I WANT LESS...   DATE

Manifestation Board

WRITE DOWN WHAT YOU WANT TO MANIFEST THIS SEASON SIS,
DREAM BIG AND BELIEVE.

LET'S DISCUSS YOUR INNER CHILD. IN THIS GENTLE WELLBEING EXERCISE DESCRIBE YOUR INNER CHILD. BE DETAILED, BE HONEST + INCLUDE HOW THEY ARE FEELING AT THIS EXACT MOMENT.

WRITE A LETTER TO YOUR INNER CHILD; WHAT DOES SHE NEED? HOW DOES SHE FEEL? HOW CAN YOU SOOTHE HER?

MAKE SOME NOTES ON HOW YOU ARE GOING SHOW UP FOR YOUR INNER CHILD MORE OFTEN.

Date: _____

Reset, Reflect, Revive

Read the prompts below and respond by filling each space provided using the initial words, phrases or sentences that come into mind.

What 3 things went well for me today?

What 2 things could I do better today?

What 1 thing can I do differently tomorrow?

What am I feeling in this moment? What have I learnt about myself today?

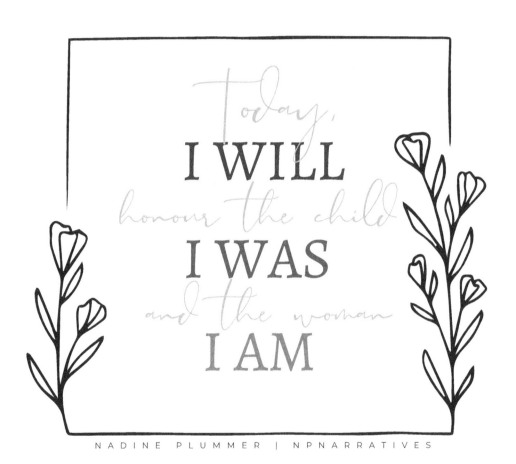

Today,
I WILL
honour the child
I WAS
and the woman
I AM

Meditation
Inner Child Connection

Take this time to pause, to breathe and connect with parts of yourself that you may neglect, overlook or have never consciously aligned with.

SECONDS

Find a comfortable position, either seated with feet firmly on the ground or laying down with your head supported. Relax your jaw, remove your tongue from the roof of your mouth, part your teeth slightly. Close your eyes and listen to your natural breathing. Slowly begin to breathe in deeply for 4 seconds through your nose, hold for 2 seconds and exhale for 6 seconds through your mouth. Repeat. Breathe into the parts of your body that feel tense/tight. Breathe oxygen into those areas. Soothe them.

Allow your breathing to return to its normal state of being. Now that you are more relaxed envision a golden thread in front of you. Take hold of this thread and follow it to its destination. You see a small figure. A silhouette of a child; your inner child. The golden thread connects you together. Now you are both enveloped in this aura of golden light. You can feel her warmth. You find yourself face-to-face with your inner child. You embrace her.

This embrace allows you to feel what your inner child is feeling. You can clearly hear her soft whispers. She tells you what she needs. You listen intently and with each acknowledgement you hug your inner child a littler tighter. Allow any emotions that you feel to come to the surface. Take note of them. Settle into this stillness and calm with this version of Self. Continue to let your breathing happen naturally. Do not force anything. Flow as freely as the golden light that surrounds you both.

As you step back from your inner child you leave enough space between you to feel her energy. Speak affirming words to her that will hold space for her until your return again. Slowly step backwards, allow the golden thread to break free from your grasp. Take a deep breathe in through your nose for 4 seconds, hold for 2 seconds, audibly exhale for 6 seconds, repeat 5 times. Slowly begin to wiggle your feet and fingers. Flutter open your eyes. Remain still for a few seconds before you rise. Give yourself a hug and say I AM LOVED.

I require...

MORE OF

LESS OF

SOME OF

NONE OF

I AM SHOWING UP FOR MYSELF BY...

I AM HOLDING MYSELF ACCOUNTABLE BY...

I AM HOLDING SPACE FOR MYSELF BY...

Areas of Improvement

Use this template to help you keep list areas of your life that you feel require your time, dedication and attention. Be honest with yourself, that is the only way you will improve these areas moving forward.

TODAY I FEEL

1 _____
_____
_____

2 _____
_____
_____

3 _____
_____
_____

4 _____
_____
_____

5 _____
_____
_____

6 _____
_____
_____

7 _____
_____
_____

8 _____
_____
_____

9 _____
_____
_____

10 _____
_____
_____

TOMORROW I WILL   I WANT MORE...   I WANT LESS...   DATE

expectation
/ek-spek-tey-shuhn/ noun

1. The act of anticipating or looking forward
2. The likelihood that something will occur/happen
3. The prospect of future prosperity

My soul wants to surrender the idea of expectations.
The ones I have set for myself and the ones I try to bend my back
limboing under for others. It is time to let my roots that ground me
travel and transcend beyond my own sight. What is mine is meant
for me and me alone. To remove the umbrella that shields me from
the rain is a gift to myself to find the peace within the storm. To
steady the pace of my heart. To release the tension that lies knotted
between the edges of my shoulder blades is a freedom I choose to
exist in. Surrendering expectation does not mean that I no longer
have dreams, goals and aspirations; instead it means to let go of
the pressure and anxiety that comes with its crippling
condemnation. I let the rainfall wash over me. I can breathe
without the burden of the expectancy weighing down on my lungs.
I know I am yet to master this, but peace arrives with patience and
joy in the morning.
I will continue to let go of it all moment by moment, day by day.

Time to Surrender

USE THE SECTIONS BELOW TO LIST YOUR NEEDS, WANTS, GOALS AND HAVES.

NEEDS

WANTS

GOALS

HAVES

WRITE DOWN A PRAYER THAT EMBODIES YOUR
FAITH IN THE PROCESS...

WRITE A LETTER OF GRATITUDE FOR A MOMENT THAT BROUGHT YOU JOY...

Meditation
Manifestation Breathwork

Take this time to pause, to breathe and connect with parts of yourself that you may neglect, overlook or have never consciously aligned with.

SECONDS

Settle down in a space that does not have a lot of distractions. Get comfortable for the next few minutes. For this period of time you are focusing on your breath. Take a deep inhale through your nose for 7 seconds, hold for 7 seconds and exhale for 7 seconds through your mouth. With each inhalation think of what desires you want to manifest and with each exhalation repeat the words 'Thank You Universe/God/Source/Ancestors' in your mind. Repeat for 2 minutes.

Remember, at this moment nothing else matters. Acknowledge your thoughts but do not engage with them. This is your time to visualise.

For the next 30 seconds allow for your breathing to return to its naturally pace. What feelings rose to the surface? Do you feel at ease? Are you feeling calm and peaceful? Were you able to visualise your intended manifestation(s)?

Gift yourself with a final minute of stillness. Begin to inhale for 5 seconds through your nose, hold for 5 seconds and the release an audible exhale for 5 seconds through your mouth. When you do your exhalation breathe out any limiting thoughts that are holding you back from manifesting your desires. Once the minute is up, you can choose to continue doing the breathwork or you can slowly bring yourself back into your space.

EVERY DAY OFFERS ME THE OPPOTUNITY TO...

I RAISE MY VIBRATIONS BY DOING THE FOLLOWING PRACTICES...

Be Grateful
Be Thankful
Be Open

Use this template to help you keep track of all the wonderful things/people you are grateful for in life.

Be clear Sis! Use your gratitude list as a way of creating journal prompts; why you are grateful for this particular thing/person?

TODAY I FEEL

1 _____
_____
_____
_____

2 _____
_____
_____
_____

3 _____
_____
_____

4 _____
_____
_____

5 _____
_____
_____

6 _____
_____
_____

7 _____
_____
_____

8 _____
_____
_____

9 _____
_____
_____

10 _____
_____
_____

TOMORROW I WILL   I WANT MORE...   I WANT LESS...   DATE

EVERY DAY IS AN OPPORTUNITY TO

grow

Date: _____

Reset, Reflect, Revive

Read the prompts below and respond by filling each space provided using the initial words, phrases or sentences that come into mind.

What 3 things went well for me today?	What 2 things could I do better today?

What 1 thing can I do differently tomorrow?	What am I feeling in this moment? What have I learnt about myself today?

affirmation
/af-er-mey-shuhn/ noun

1. State of being affirmed
2. A clear statement that is declared to be true
3. Confirmation of the truth
4. To assert that something exists

Today I don't want to be strong, I want to be soft and malleable.
Today I don't want to be brave, I want to be rescued and held close
to my heart.
Today I want to be visible, I do not want to be under covers of my
bed hiding until the sun rises again.
Today I want to be outspoken, whilst leaning into being quiet as I
settle into my silence; searching for moments of peace.
Today I want to laugh out loud, I want to let my tears waterfall
from my eyes and pool on the apples of my
cheeks as a form of release.
Today I want to be a lover, I want to let my enriching emotions
merge with one another until one of them reigns victorious.
Today I don't want to be your version of me.
Today I want to be Me.

I AM...

w o r t h y

WHAT SETS YOUR SOUL ON FIRE? ARE YOU PURSUING THIS VENTURE? HOW DOES IT FEEL?

I am choosing a path that allows me to pursue my dream of

THE AFFIRMATION THAT SPEAKS TO MY SOUL THE MOST THIS SEASON IS_____ BECAUSE....

Live a life of **gratitude**, its the most favorable **attitude** that there is.

Self-Care Board

NOTE DOWN YOUR FAVOURITE ACTS OF SELF CARE

Date: _____

Reset, Reflect, Revive

Read the prompts below and respond by filling each space provided using the initial words, phrases or sentences that come into mind.

What 3 things went well for me today?	What 2 things could I do better today?

What 1 thing can I do differently tomorrow?	What am I feeling in this moment? What have I learnt about myself today?

substitute temporary
happiness for

joy
/joi/ noun

1. An emotion that represents great delight which has been caused by something exceptionally good/satisfying
2. A state of felicity
3. A source of pleasure

I watch she stirring the stew chicken in the dutch pot
The sweet aroma fills the air in the cubicle sized kitchen
Calypso whispering to her hips as she sways them in a figure of eight
Hard beats and soft whines
Transporting me to the "small island"
Mystical blue seas
Shimmering sunlight graduating into a hazy sunset
The waves rolling as effortlessly as she waistline
I sit there
Picking the peas
Mother & daughter dancing in the sunday ritual
Of cooking with soul
& giving thanks to the Most High

WHAT BRINGS YOU JOY IN YOUR DAY-TO-DAY? WHAT DOES
THIS SENSE OF JOY FEEL LIKE?

JOY TASTES SWEET
IN THE MORNING,
SMOOTH IN THE
AFTERNOON AND
SATISFYING IN THE
EVENING.

LIST PEOPLE WHO YOU ARE GRATEFUL FOR BELOW. THINK ABOUT WHY YOU ARE GRATEFUL FOR THEM. WRITE THEM A LETTER/TELL THEM YOUR FEELINGS.

I FIND MY JOY IN MOMENTS THAT STEM FROM...

Meditation
Body Scan

Take this time to pause, to breathe and connect with parts of yourself that you may neglect, overlook or have never consciously aligned with.

SECONDS

Find a comfortable position, either seated with feet firmly on the ground or laying down with head supported. Relax your jaw, remove your tongue from the roof of your mouth, part your teeth slightly. Place your left hand on your womb space and your right hand on your heart. Close your eyes and listen to your natural breathing. Listen to your heartbeat. Slowly begin to breathe in deeply for 4 seconds through your nose, hold for 4 seconds and exhale for 6 seconds through your mouth. Repeat.

Start from the tips of your toes, pay attention to any sensations that you are feeling. Slowly move up to your calves, your knees, then your thighs. Take a moment to pause. Continue to travel up to your pelvic area. Allow yourself some time to focus on your womb space. *What emotions are you holding in this space?* Move onto your stomach, chest, heart space. Pause. *What are you feeling?* Continue with your finger tips, palms of hands, lower arms, elbows, shoulders glide over your neck, take a moment to explore your back area. Start to soften your mouth, tongue, cheeks, eyes. Allow the energy to escape through your crown. Allow what is not serving you to leave your body. Continue to let your breathing fill your belly. On your exhalations draw your belly button towards your back. Do not be forceful, be *graceful*.

Spend a moment allowing your body to sink deeper into its surroundings. Allow your breath to resume its natural steady pace. Speak three of your affirmations to yourself three times. Slowly begin to move your fingers and toes. Flutter your eyes open. Slowly rise.

THERE ARE A MILLION AND ONE REASONS TO FEEL DEFEATED, UNEASY, AND UNCERATIN RIGHT NOW, BUT WHEN YOU ARE ONE IN A MILLION, YOU AREN'T AFRAID OF FEELING A LITTLE UNCOMFORTABLE IN ORDER TO REACH YOUR SWEET SPOT.

don't forget

YOU'VE GOT THIS SIS!

Date: _____

Reset, Reflect, Revive

Read the prompts below and respond by filling each space provided using the initial words, phrases or sentences that come into mind.

What 3 things went well for me today?

What 2 things could I do better today?

What 1 thing can I do differently tomorrow?

What am I feeling in this moment? What have I learnt about myself today?

awareness

/uh-wair-nis/ noun

1. A state of being aware
2. Having knowledge
3. Being conscious

Dear Black Woman

Your life matters. It may ache from being stretched too thin, but it is yours. Your life matters because without it there would be no Us. I see the pain in your eyes, that lingers round your black pupils. You are a reflection of the woman I see in the mirror. We have experienced the highs and lows together on different timelines. We have endured the trials and tribulations of assimilation. Scrapping away to belong at tables that did not see us fit to be there but were welcoming of our ability to wait. Often having to settle into the coarseness of rejection from our homes, our colleagues, and our men. Yet our soul's needs and wants exemplifies that we are deserving of so much more.

Dear Black Woman

Be brave in all you do. Let the wind carry you to your destination. Allow yourself to heal, to feel, to release all that you are in the world that tries its best not to see you or acknowledge your existence as Mother Earth. You are worth it and more. A diamond encased in gold. You shine. Lighting up rooms, as you trail-blaze through the atmosphere. Nothing can stand in your way as your roots are firmly planted, transcending the land, extending towards your purpose. Transform during this transition. Excel in this period of elevation and evolution. Seek the Self that scream to rise to the surface.

Let me see your beauty.

TODAY I AM AWARE OF THE FACT THAT THE WOMAN I WAS YESTERDAY WAS NOT QUALIFIED TO/WAS QUALIFIED TO...

USE THE SECTIONS BELOW TO LIST YOUR NEEDS, WANTS, GOALS AND HAVES.

NEEDS

WANTS

GOALS

HAVES

I AM AWARE OF MY INTERNAL BEAUTY

I AM RADIATING
MY BEAUTY EXTERNALLY

NADINE PLUMMER | NPNARRATIVES

I HAVE LEARNT THAT I AM A WOMAN WHO LIVES HER LIFE BY...

I LOVE THESE QUALITLIES ABOUT ME... THE QUALITIES I HAVE GROWN TO APPRECIATE ABOUT MYSELF ARE...

I AM AWARE THAT MY CUP IS AT ITS FULLEST WHEN...
I AM AWARE THAT MY CUP IS IN A STATE OF LACK WHEN...

Date: _____

Reset, Reflect, Revive

Read the prompts below and respond by filling each space provided using the initial words, phrases or sentences that come into mind.

What 3 things went well for me today?

What 2 things could I do better today?

What 1 thing can I do differently tomorrow?

What am I feeling in this moment? What have I learnt about myself today?

Be gentle with yourself.

selfhood

/self-hood/ noun

1. The state of being an individual person
2. Individuality
3. Owning your uniqueness
4. A sense of your identity

The more I took the time to look at myself in the mirror of my life, the more I realised that I have always been more than I gave myself credit for. I have always been strong enough to support myself during the hardships I have endured. I have always been able to nurture and nourish myself more often than not. I have always been my biggest cheerleader in my journey towards my goals. I have always been the best version of me that I could be at any given time, even when I felt like I couldn't go on.

This is the woman that I AM.

LIST 50 WORDS THAT DESCRIBE YOU IN A POSITIVE LIGHT

Let Go of the Negative Self-Talk

WHAT FALSE NARRATIVES ARE YOU LIMITING YOURSELF WITH? LIST THEM HERE AND THINK ABOUT HOW YOU CAN REFRAME THEM.

AS I LEAN INTO THE WOMAN THAT I AM BECOMING, I AM CONFIDENT THAT I WILL...

I BELIEVE IN MYSELF MOST WHEN... THEREFORE I WILL DO MORE OF THIS IN ORDER TO MAINTAIN THIS LEVEL OF SELF-WORTH.

USE THE SECTIONS BELOW TO LIST YOUR NEEDS, WANTS, GOALS AND HAVES.

NEEDS

WANTS

GOALS

HAVES

Meditation
Explore Your Senses

Take this time to pause, to breathe and connect with parts of yourself that you may neglect, overlook or have never consciously aligned with.

SECONDS

Find a comfortable position, either seated with feet firmly on the ground or laying down with head supported. Relax your jaw, remove your tongue from the roof of your mouth, part your teeth slightly. Allow your breath to be smooth and easy. Do not focus so much on the pace, allow it to flow naturally. Let this be the time to release any heaviness that you might have been carrying around with you throughout the day.

Take the time to let your senses be hyperactive. Choose a sense that you want to explore with first. For example, what can you **hear**; can you hear voices in the other room, the sound of the tv, the echoing of the birds outside or the sound of cars driving by? Overlay this with the sense of **smell**; what aromas can you smell within your space? Is it the floral scents of a candle, food cooking in the kitchen. Could it be the perfume that you are wearing?

Go through each scent. Do not rush. Aim for at least 4-5 minutes of just giving yourself the freedom to connect immediate space through your senses.

Let yourself bask in the stillness of Self.

Slowly arrive back into the room. Focus your attention to your breathing. Start to move your body slowly. Do not rush out of your position. Open your eyes and let yourself succumb to a feeling of calm. How do you feel?

THE GIRL I WAS BELIEVED THAT...

Date: _____

Reset, Reflect, Revive

Read the prompts below and respond by filling each space provided using the initial words, phrases or sentences that come into mind.

What 3 things went well for me today?

What 2 things could I do better today?

What 1 thing can I do differently tomorrow?

What am I feeling in this moment? What have I learnt about myself today?

THE WOMAN THAT I AM HAS LEARNT THAT...

THE QUEEN THAT I AM BECOMING KNOWS THAT...

Date: _____

Reset, Reflect, Revive

Read the prompts below and respond by filling each space provided using the initial words, phrases or sentences that come into mind.

What 3 things went well for me today?	What 2 things could I do better today?

What 1 thing can I do differently tomorrow?	What am I feeling in this moment? What have I learnt about myself today?

Reminder

To know yourself is to love
yourself wholeheartedly.

JOURNAL PROMPTS

Use these bonus journal prompts to help you go a little further inwards.

Set aside 10-20 minutes each day to complete one of the suggested prompts.

JOURNAL PROMPTS FOR SELF-LOVE

I love my body because...

I have learnt to adore this _____about myself, and now I feel more...

I am healing my wound of....

JOURNAL PROMPTS FOR CONFIDENCE

What am I good at?

My strengths are...

List your talents, traits and triumphs, what does this say about you as a person?

I feel at my most confident when...

JOURNAL PROMPTS FOR GROWTH

What is my learning style?

How can I manage my time in order to maximize my productivity?

What can I let go of so that I can create space for new opportunities?

JOURNAL PROMPTS FOR YOUR INNER CHILD

I am most playful when...

My favourite childhood memory is...

I find joy in doing...

I am feel free when I am....

JOURNAL PROMPTS FOR FORGIVENESS

What one thing do you need to forgive yourself for? Why is it important to give yourself forgiveness?

What does forgiveness mean to you?

Who do you need to forgive? Write a letter to that person and then dispose of it.

About the Author

Nadine Plummer is a mother, wife, daughter and sister who prides herself on being a woman of integrity, compassion and empathy. In 2020, she decided to intentionally connect with other Black/Brown woman in the hopes of creating a solid foundation of sisterhood and support. Her conversations with women who looked like her and reflected her experiences led to Nadine's decision to marry up her love of writing, desire for community and acts of service together. From applying her lessons learnt through her own personal traumas and triumphs, Nadine was able to cultivate a space that offers inspiration, realisation, manifestations, empowerment, healing and comfort to other women of colour.

Nadine has already helped over a hundred women elevate to the next level of their personal development journeys, and continues to make great strides in providing services (courses, workshops, and resources) that gifts Black/Brown women with new ways to honour the beautiful, bountiful beings that they are outside of the generic labels that have been placed upon them.

Connect with Nadine on
@npnarratives
www.npnarratives.com

Printed in Great Britain
by Amazon

22613961R00057